WOMEN AT WAR: THE PROGRESSIVE ERA, WORLD WAR I, AND WOMEN'S SUFFRAGE 1900–1920

JANE BINGHAM

CHELSEA HOUSE
An Infobase Learning Company

WOMEN AT WAR: THE PROGRESSIVE ERA, WORLD WAR I, AND WOMEN'S SUFFRAGE 1900–1920

Copyright © 2011 Bailey Publishing Associates Ltd

Produced for Chelsea House by Bailey Publishing Associates Ltd, 11a Woodlands, Hove BN3 6TJ, England

Library of Congress Cataloging-in-Publication Data

Bingham, Jane.
   Women at war : the progressive era, World War I and women's suffrage, 1900–1920 / Jane Bingham.
      p. cm. — (A cultural history of women in America)
   Includes index.
   ISBN 978-1-60413-932-7
   1. Women—United States—History—20th century. 2. World War, 1914–1918—United States. 3. Women—Employment—United States— History—20th century. 4. Women—United States—Social conditions—20th century. 5. Women—Political activity—United States—History— 20th century. I. Title. II. Series.

HQ1419.B56 2011
305.40973'09041—dc22
                                    2010044828

Chelsea House books are available at special discounts when purchased in bulk quantities for businesses, associations, institutions, or sales promotions. Please call our Special Sales Department in New York at (212) 967-8800 or (800) 322-8755.

You can find Chelsea House on the World Wide Web at http://www.chelseahouse.com

Project management by Patience Coster
Text design by Jane Hawkins
Picture research by Shelley Noronha
Printed and bound in Malaysia
Bound book date: April 2011

10 9 8 7 6 5 4 3 2 1

This book is printed on acid-free paper.

All links and Web addresses were checked and verified to be correct at the time of publication. Because of the dynamic nature of the Web, some addresses and links may have changed since publication and may no longer be valid.

The publishers would like to thank the following for permission to reproduce their photographs:
The Art Archive: 13 (Culver Pictures), 25 (Museum of the City of New York /43.40.128), 44 (Museum of the City of New York /MCNY93), 45 (Museum of the City of New York /37.361.67), 50 (National Archives, Washington D.C.); Corbis: 6, 10, 11 (Lake County Museum), 14, 15 (Bettmann), 17 (Bettmann), 19 (Bettmann), 20, 21 (Bettmann), 23 (Underwood & Underwood), 24 (Bettmann), 27, 28 (Hulton-Deutsch Collection), 29 (Lake County Museum), 31, 32 (Hulton-Deutsch Collection), 33 (Bettmann), 43 (Underwood & Underwood), 46 (Bettmann), 47 (Bettmann), 48 (EFE), 51, 52, 55 (Bettmann), 57 (Bettmann), 58, 59 (Bettmann/ Collection of the New-York Historical Society); Getty Images: 8, 9, 12, 34, 37, 40, 54, 56; The Library of Congress: 7, 16, 18, 22, 26, 30, 35, 38, 39, 41, 42, 49 (Harris & Ewing Collection); National Archives: 5 (War & Conflict no.544); TopFoto: 36 (The Granger Collection), 53 (The Granger Collection).

CONTENTS

Between the years 1900 to 1920, life changed dramatically for many women in the United States. Growing numbers of women were employed outside the home, especially during World War I. There were breakthroughs for women in the fields of sports, music, business, and the arts. It was also a period of social concern, when some courageous women led campaigns to make a difference to others' lives.

This book concentrates on key areas of women's lives, such as their role in the family and the workplace. It looks at the part some women played in World War I and traces the struggle of the suffragists to win the right to vote. It also follows the many campaigns for social reform organized by remarkable women such as Jane Addams, Margaret Sanger, and Ida Wells-Barnett.

The United States in the early years of the 20th century was a place of great social contrast. This book surveys the lives of the poor as well as the rich, including less privileged groups, such as African Americans. While most women gained more rights in the period 1900 to 1920, some continued to face discrimination and injustice.

Right: Women took over men's jobs when the troops went off to fight in World War I. During the war years, many American women gained new skills as factory workers.

TURNING POINT

THE 19TH AMENDMENT

On August 26, 1920, the 19th Amendment to the Constitution of the United States became law. This amendment granted all women the right to vote. It was the goal of a long, drawn-out campaign for women's suffrage that had begun in the 19th century. After many years of struggle, women were finally recognized as full citizens of the United States.

CHAPTER I

AN ERA OF CHANGE

THE PERIOD 1900 TO 1920 WAS A TIME OF DRAMATIC upheaval and disruption. During these years, there was a catastrophic world war, and communism was born. It was also a time of social change. As industries and cities grew rapidly, traditional patterns of family life began to break down.

TURNING POINT

AMERICA GOES TO WAR

On April 6, 1917, the United States formally entered World War I. This involvement in a distant war had several consequences for American society. Apart from the tragic loss of young lives, the absence of young men from the workforce provided a chance for women to perform a range of jobs. At the same time, women's involvement in the war effort helped to gain public support for the campaign for female voting rights.

Right: All American citizens were encouraged to contribute to the war effort. This poster was used to advertise Victory Liberty Loans, a form of savings certificate. Money raised from the loans helped to fund the United States' contribution to World War I.

WORLD WAR I

World War I broke out in June 1914. It started with a conflict between two rival groups of nations: Germany and Austro-Hungary on one side and Britain, France, and Russia (a group sometimes called the Allies) on the other. Soon other countries had joined the war. Turkey and Bulgaria supported Germany, while Italy, Greece, and Portugal joined the Allies. Most of the fighting took place in France and Belgium (known as the Western Front).

Both sides tried to prevent food and other supplies from reaching their enemies. This meant German submarines, known as U-boats, attacked all ships heading for Britain. When some American ships were attacked by U-boats, President Woodrow Wilson decided that the United States should join the war on the side of the Allies. From April 1917, American troops fought alongside the Allies until the end of the war in November 1918. By then, sixty-five million people had been killed. More than 126,000 Americans died, and 234,000 were wounded.

THE RUSSIAN REVOLUTION

In Russia in 1917, Vladimir Ilyich Lenin led an uprising of workers and peasants against their all-powerful ruler, the czar. Lenin and his Bolshevik Party seized control of Russia and introduced a totally new system of government. The Bolsheviks removed Russia's ruling class, gave land to the peasants and put the workers in charge of their factories. This marked the start of the communist system.

In Europe and the United States, some radical thinkers were inspired by what was happening in Russia and attempted to make some drastic social changes of their own. Anarchists such as Emma Goldman campaigned for social reform but also plotted to overthrow society completely.

Right: Emma Goldman emigrated from Russia to the United States when she was sixteen years old. She campaigned tirelessly for workers' rights.

WOMEN ENTER THE WORKPLACE

"*There has been a sudden influx of women into such unusual occupations as bank clerks, ticket sellers, elevator operator, chauffeur, street car conductor, railroad trackwalker, section hand, locomotive wiper and oiler, locomotive dispatcher, block operator, draw bridge attendant, and employment in machine shops, steel mills, powder and ammunition factories, airplane works, boot blacking and farming.*"

An extract from the *Seattle Union Record*, April 24, 1918, illustrates how women's lives changed as they took on men's jobs when soldiers left to fight in World War I.

7

Right: The Flatiron Building in New York was completed in 1902 and was one of the city's first skyscrapers. It was given its nickname because its shape resembled an iron for smoothing clothes.

IMMIGRATION TO THE UNITED STATES

Poverty, war, and disruption in Europe led to mass emigration to the United States. Most of the immigrants came from eastern and southern Europe and arrived in the United States full of hope, in search of new opportunities. In 1907, immigration from Europe reached its peak, with 1,285,349 people entering the United States.

INDUSTRY AND TRANSPORT

The early 20th century was a period of rapid industrial growth in the United States. Most American cities had steel mills and textile factories as well as numerous clothing workshops. Factories produced a wide range of consumer goods, which were sold in the new department stores.

The construction industry flourished in the cities as wealthy industrialists paid for exciting new "skyscrapers." Transportation also expanded in this period. Railroad companies built new tracks across the United States, and most cities had a streetcar system. By 1900,

Oldsmobile were manufacturing automobiles, and in 1908, Henry Ford launched his hugely popular Model T Ford—the first automobile that ordinary American families could afford. In 1900, Americans owned 8,000 automobiles. In 1920, there were eight million automobile owners in the United States.

AN UNEQUAL SOCIETY

With the growth of industrial society, the problems of the poor became more obvious. Drawn by the prospect of employment, many people moved to the cities, while immigrants arrived by the thousands in search of work. Most of these people lived in slum districts in crowded, dangerous, and unsanitary conditions. Workers were often exploited, working for up to fourteen hours a day for very little pay.

Some ethnic groups faced particular difficulties. African Americans were frequently treated as second-class citizens, while Native Americans were forced off their land and sent to live on reservations.

THE PROGRESSIVE MOVEMENT

The period from 1890 to 1920 is sometimes known as the Progressive Era because of the many individuals and groups who tried to achieve positive "progress" within their society. "Progressive" campaigners were mainly educated, middle-class men and women who recognized that their society faced some very serious problems, created by industrialization, urbanization, and immigration. They aimed to find solutions to these problems, campaigning for workers' rights, safety at work, and improved facilities for education and public health. Women fought for the right to vote, and some Progressives worked toward achieving equal treatment for people of all races.

A few outstanding Progressives tackled social problems themselves, setting up their own social welfare organizations, such as "settlement houses" in poor urban neighborhoods. They also persuaded the government to provide more social support and to make some important changes to the law.

WOMEN OF COURAGE AND CONVICTION

JANE ADDAMS (1860–1935)

In 1889, Jane Addams moved into Hull-House, in a poor, industrial district of Chicago. Her aim was to create a lively civic center, which could offer education, friendship, and support for the local community. Within a couple of years, Hull-House was attracting up to 2,000 people a week. Men, women, and children came to the "settlement house" to attend classes, enjoy the leisure facilities, and receive help with medical, legal, and other problems. Jane Addams lived in Hull-House right up until her death. She was a tireless campaigner for social reform and a passionate pacifist. In 1931, she became the first American woman to be awarded the Nobel Peace Prize.

Below: Jane Addams was only twenty-nine when she founded Hull-House. Others quickly followed her example, and almost five hundred settlement houses were established in American cities over the next thirty years.

CHAPTER 2

FAMILY AND SOCIETY

I N THE EARLY 20TH CENTURY, WOMEN BEGAN TO SPEND MORE TIME outside the home. For those with money and education, this was a positive experience since many of them found rewarding work or formed women's clubs and associations. Poorer women had a hard time, working very long hours and struggling to combine their roles as wives, mothers, and workers. Some wealthy women took measures to assist their less fortunate sisters, forming groups to support the vulnerable and campaigning for birth control to help to reduce family size.

CHANGING FAMILIES

With the rise of industrialized society, patterns of family life began to change. In poorer families, it was common for both husbands and wives to go out to work in factories, leaving their children alone for long periods. The rapid increase in factory jobs resulted in a move away from domestic service, and this had an impact on wealthier families. Many middle-class women found themselves without domestic help and had to learn how to do their own housework. With their husbands usually out at work, middle-class wives had most of the responsibility for raising their children too.

In addition to these changes in family life, there was a steep increase in the rate of divorce. A report published in

Left: Women were often employed in textile factories, doing repetitive manual tasks. These women are working in a silk mill, sorting and cleaning fibers from silkworm cocoons.

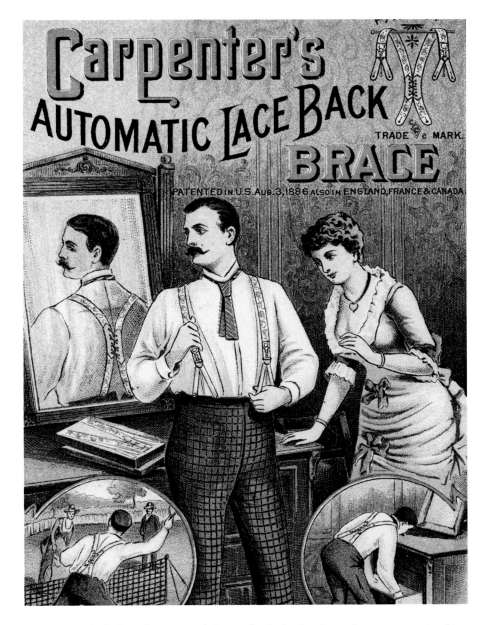

TURNING POINT

THE BRA IS BORN

In 1913, Mary Phelps Jacob invented the brassiere, which she created with the help of her maid using two silk handkerchiefs and some ribbon. The following year, she sold her idea to Warner Brothers Corset Company for $1,500. Women were delighted by the freedom offered by the brassiere. Up until 1914, women had worn corsets, stiffened with strips of whalebone and tied at the back with laces.

Left: The image of women in the 1900s was very much that of helpmate to their husbands and families.

TURNING POINT

NEW APPLIANCES

The first completely electric washing machine was sold in 1908 by the Hurley Machine Company in Chicago. Early vacuum cleaners also began to appear in the shops in about 1910. The new household appliances were intended to make the housewife's life much easier, but advances in technology also raised standards of cleanliness. Many housewives in this period devoted most of their day to housework.

1899 revealed that the United States had the highest divorce rate in the world. Some people feared that the American ideal of the family was in danger, and this prompted many attempts at social reform.

SOCIAL REFORMS

In response to fears about the growing divorce rate, several states toughened their divorce laws, while some took measures to try to prevent bad marriages. States raised the age of consent and even passed laws outlawing marriages between men and women who suffered from drunkenness, venereal disease, addiction, or mental health problems. However, these measures were not easy to enforce, and the divorce rate continued to rise.

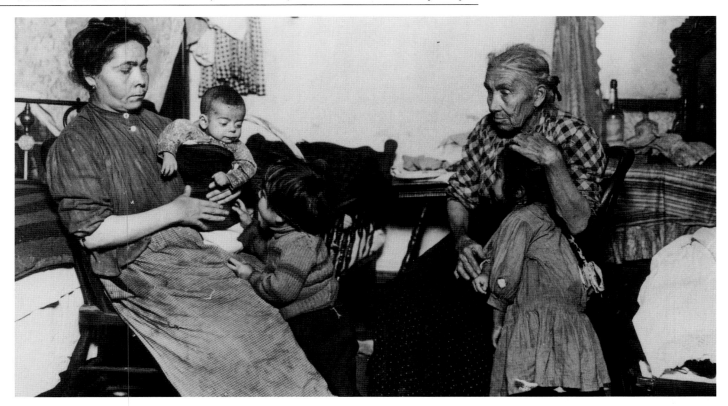

Above: For people living in poverty, each new baby meant more suffering for the whole family.

" A CALL FOR SMALLER FAMILIES

"Women of the working class, especially wage workers, should not have more than two children at the most. The average working man can support no more and the average working woman can take care of no more. It has been my experience that more children are not really wanted, but that women are compelled to have them either from lack of foresight or through ignorance . . ."

Margaret Sanger, campaigner for birth control, *Family Limitation* (1914)

Some states enforced strict school attendance laws. These were partly an attempt to remove immigrant children from their homes because educators believed that the schools provided a better environment for preparing children for American life. Within the schools, girls were given home economics classes to learn dressmaking and cooking skills.

CHILD-CARE ADVICE

Experts on child care bombarded mothers with advice on "rational" methods of child rearing. They published books and articles advising parents to set strict sleeping and eating schedules for their children. Mothers were also warned not to play with or cuddle young children because this placed a strain on a child's nervous system.

SOCIAL PROBLEMS

In the poorest districts of American cities, there was serious hardship. Families lived in badly maintained and crowded accommodations, often crammed together in a single room. Men and women worked up to fourteen hours a day for very little pay, and children as young as eight years old were often employed in factories. Without any reliable means of contraception, families were large, and parents struggled to feed and clothe all their children. In addition to these problems, many women suffered abuse from their drunken and violent husbands.

12

Above: For many, Carrie Nation was a subject of ridicule, but others saw her as a courageous campaigner against the evils of the age.

WOMEN OF COURAGE AND CONVICTION

CARRIE NATION (1846–1911)

Carrie Nation began her temperance campaigns in Kansas in the 1880s, but in 1900 she decided to adopt more radical methods. Gathering several rocks, she headed for the local saloon and began hurling them at its stock of liquor. Nation continued her saloon raids all over Kansas, using a hatchet to achieve maximum damage. She was arrested about thirty times for "hatchetations," as she called them, but managed to pay her court fines from the fees she charged for lectures and the sales of souvenir hatchets.

Some women of influence decided to use their money and power to solve the social problems they saw around them. Sometimes they worked alone, but they also founded a number of progressive clubs and associations. The aim of these women's clubs was to offer help to the needy and also to tackle the sources of their problems.

THE TEMPERANCE MOVEMENT

The oldest of the women's associations was the Women's Christian Temperance Union (WCTU). It had been formed in 1873 with the aim of banning the sale and consumption of liquor. Members of the movement saw liquor as the source of a range of social problems, including domestic violence, poverty, and crime.

In the 1900s, Carrie Nation was a leading figure in the WCTU. She believed in direct action and used a hatchet (ax) to launch her violent raids on drinking saloons. By 1910, members of the temperance movement were campaigning hard for a national ban on liquor, and in 1920 they achieved their aim, when the government passed the Prohibition Act, banning the sale, manufacture, and transportation of liquor.

CAMPAIGNS FOR BIRTH CONTROL

From 1900 to 1920 a women's movement to promote birth control grew. Leaders of the movement, Margaret Sanger and Emma Goldman, organized public rallies and campaigns through which they aimed to educate women about their options for limiting the number of children they had.

Supporters of birth control argued passionately that a high birthrate restricted women's lives and put their health in danger. They saw birth control as especially vital for poorer families, where parents struggled to feed their children and women were so desperate to avoid another pregnancy that they even resorted to life-threatening back-alley (illegal) abortions.

THE COMSTOCK ACT

The biggest obstacle facing campaigners for birth control was the Comstock Act. This federal legislation banned the circulation of obscene or immoral materials through the U.S. mail. Birth control pamphlets and devices, such as diaphragms, were seen as obscene materials. Campaigners were also prosecuted under local laws for speaking in public meetings about birth control.

TURNING POINT

A FATAL TERMINATION

The turning point in Margaret Sanger's life came in 1912, when she was working as a nurse in a poor district of New York. Sanger was called to the home of Sadie Sachs, who was very ill following an attempted abortion. Sachs begged her doctor for advice on how to avoid becoming pregnant again, but he simply joked that her husband should sleep on the roof. A few months later, Sanger was called to the apartment again, but this time Sachs was found dead after another abortion.

In 1914, Margaret Sanger published *Family Limitation*, a pamphlet on birth control. She was prosecuted under the Comstock Act but escaped to Europe the day before her trial was scheduled to begin. When she returned the next year, the prosecutor dropped the charges against her, but it was clear that her campaign to educate women would not be easy.

A BIRTH CONTROL CLINIC

On October 16, 1916, Sanger opened the first birth control clinic in the United States in Brooklyn, New York. With the help of her sister, Ethel

Left: Children in poor districts had wretched lives. This photograph shows a young girl from Alabama who combined the tasks of working in a shellfish cannery with caring for her younger sister.

Left: This photograph, taken in 1916, shows Margaret Sanger outside the courthouse where she was on trial for sending a book on contraception through the mail.

Byrne, she provided advice to nearly five hundred women before the police closed down the clinic ten days later. Sanger was put on trial for breaking the New York law banning distribution of birth control information and was given a thirty-day jail sentence.

Sanger tried a different approach the following year. The Comstock Act allowed doctors to give information on birth control to a married person in order to cure or prevent a disease. She therefore began to open a series of clinics staffed by doctors. Sanger also published a more moderate magazine, *Birth Control Review*, which she used to express her views and to make connections with the medical community.

THE VOLUNTARY PARENTHOOD LEAGUE

Mary Ware Dennett also supported birth control, but she took a different approach from Margaret Sanger. Dennett did not support clinics staffed by doctors because they failed to reach the poorest women in society. Instead she concentrated on trying to change the

WOMEN OF COURAGE AND CONVICTION

MARY WARE DENNETT (1872–1947)

Mary Ware Dennett was a suffragist, a pacifist, and a talented craftswoman, but she is best known as a campaigner for birth control and sex education. In addition to leading the Voluntary Parenthood League, Dennett wrote a pamphlet on sex education for teenagers. *The Sex Side of Life* was published in 1918 and circulated widely to youth and church organizations and state health departments before being banned as obscene in 1922. Dennett was tried under the Comstock Act in 1928 and fined $300. Two years later, following a nationwide public protest, the U.S. Court of Appeals reversed the judgment against Dennett and pronounced that the Comstock Act should not "interfere with serious instruction regarding sex matters."

WOMEN OF COURAGE AND CONVICTION

LILLIAN WALD (1867–1940)

Lillian Wald trained as a nurse before moving to a poor district of New York. At first, she worked in an orphanage, but soon she was caring for sick residents of the Lower East Side as a visiting nurse. In 1893, she founded the Henry Street Settlement House, which she used as a base for her nursing service. By 1913, she had a staff of ninety-two nurses. Wald was especially concerned with child health and welfare. She sent visiting nurses into schools, campaigned against child labor, and helped to establish the Children's Bureau.

Below: In addition to working as a nurse, Lillian Wald was an activist for peace, a teacher, an author, a publisher, and a vigorous campaigner for civil rights.

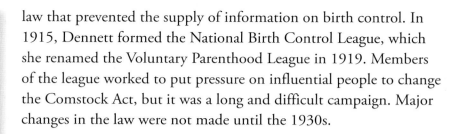

law that prevented the supply of information on birth control. In 1915, Dennett formed the National Birth Control League, which she renamed the Voluntary Parenthood League in 1919. Members of the league worked to put pressure on influential people to change the Comstock Act, but it was a long and difficult campaign. Major changes in the law were not made until the 1930s.

SETTLEMENT HOUSES

The settlement house movement began in the 1880s in response to the conditions in poor urban neighborhoods. Groups of educated men and women moved to run-down districts and established houses where they lived alongside poor residents and tried to improve their lives. By 1900, more than one hundred settlement houses had been established, mostly in the large industrial cities of the Northeast and Midwest, and most of them were run by women.

JANE ADDAMS AT HULL-HOUSE

The earliest settlement house was founded by Jane Addams in 1889, in a poor district of Chicago. At first, only Addams and her college friend, Ellen Gates Starr, lived in Hull-House, but it soon became home to twenty-five women. By 1911, the Hull-House complex consisted of thirteen buildings, and in 1912, a summer camp was added.

Volunteers at Hull-House held free classes for all the people of the neighborhood, teaching literature, history, and art as well as domestic skills such as sewing. There were kindergartens, clubs for older children, and music and drama groups; there was also a gym, a bathhouse, and a library. The women of Hull-House nursed the sick, delivered babies, and offered shelter to women who had suffered domestic violence. Within a few years, the house had become a center for political campaigns to improve public housing, education, and health care; to stand up against unjust employers; and to protect immigrants from unfair treatment.

CAMPAIGNING FOR CHILDREN

Some women reformers concentrated their efforts on improving the lives of children. They were very concerned about the future health of boys and girls

THE CHILDREN OF HULL-HOUSE

"Our very first Christmas at Hull-House, when we as yet knew nothing of child labor, a number of little girls refused the candy which was offered them as part of the Christmas good cheer, saying simply that they "worked in a candy factory and could not bear the sight of it." We discovered that for six weeks they had worked from seven in the morning until nine at night, and they were exhausted as well as satiated [full]."

An extract from *Twenty Years at Hull-House*, by Jane Addams

Left: Visiting nurses leaving the Henry Street settlement house on New York's Lower East Side. The nurses all lived in the Henry Street house and worked in the local community.

who had endured a miserable childhood. What could the future hold, they asked, for children who had been forced to work from an early age, who lived in unsanitary conditions, and who were malnourished and uneducated?

Two leading figures in the campaign to improve children's lives were Florence Kelley and Lillian Wald. Together they led a national campaign to develop a federal agency that would promote the health and welfare of children. The campaign took over six years, but finally in 1912, the Children's Bureau was formed. The bureau conducted research into such issues as infant mortality, child labor, diseases of children, and sanitation. It also published pamphlets giving advice to parents.

CHAPTER 3

WOMEN AT WORK

URING THE EARLY 20TH CENTURY, THE PROPORTION OF WOMEN in the workplace rose sharply. Between the years 1890 and 1900, the numbers of female workers had doubled, and this number increased by 50 percent between 1900 and 1910. A large proportion of these new female workers were employed in factories, and many of them suffered terrible working conditions. Outraged by the sufferings of female factory workers, some progressive women leaders decided to take action. Early protests included consumer pressure and legal cases. Later, protesters began to form unions and to organize strikes and marches.

HOT WORK

"We have women working in the foundries, stripped to the waist, if you please, because of the heat. . . . Of course, you know the reason they are employed in foundries is that they are cheaper and work longer hours than men. Women in the laundries, for instance, stand for 13 or 14 hours in the terrible steam and heat with their hands in hot starch. There is no harder contest than the contest for bread, let me tell you that."

An extract from a speech by Rose Schneiderman, campaigner for labor reforms

Right: Young women working at a cotton mill in Augusta, Georgia, in 1909. Women and girls employed in textile mills had to stand for hours on end, performing tiring and repetitive tasks.

Above: Women working in a gramophone factory around 1905. Male supervisors made sure the female workers kept up a constant speed of production.

WORKING CONDITIONS

Working conditions for women in factories were generally appalling. In the clothing industry, women and girls often worked a twelve-hour day, six or even seven days a week. Workers were crowded into buildings that were badly maintained, dimly lit, and often dangerous. After just a few years in the textile industry, most garment workers suffered from back problems and failing eyesight.

Most of the female factory workers were recent immigrants, who needed to support their families, and some ruthless employers took advantage of them. Without any unions to support them, these women were in a desperate situation.

CONSUMER LEAGUES

In 1899, a group of progressive women decided to form a pressure group to force employers to treat their workers more fairly. The National Consumers League urged homemakers to purchase their clothes and household goods only from companies and stores

BREAKTHROUGH BIOGRAPHY

CRYSTAL EASTMAN (1881–1928)

Crystal Eastman was one of many educated women who campaigned for workers' rights. Her first job, after she earned a law degree in 1907, was to investigate working conditions in the city of Pittsburgh, Pennsylvania. In 1910, she published *Work Accidents and the Law*, a report that became a classic and is still in print. In the same year, as the first woman member of New York State's Employers' Liability Commission, Eastman drafted the first workers' compensation law. Three years later, she became investigating attorney for the U.S. Commission on Industrial Relations. She campaigned constantly for safe working conditions until her early death at age forty-seven.

Above: Members of the Women's Trade Union League (WTUL) meet at their second conference held in Chicago, Illinois, in 1909.

that met what it called "Standards of a Fair House." These standards included wages of at least $6.00 per week (some employers paid as little as $2.50 per week), a working day that lasted no longer than 8 a.m. to 6 p.m., a forty-five-minute lunch break, an annual week's vacation with pay, and no child labor.

The league published "white lists" of companies that met their standards, and all other companies were blacklisted. Later, the plan was extended to factories: manufacturers approved by the league could win the right to attach a "white label" to their products.

FORMING UNIONS

In the opening years of the 20th century, several unions were formed to campaign for female workers' rights. The International Ladies' Garment Workers' Union (ILGWU) was founded in New York City in 1900 to improve conditions for textile workers. However, few women workers joined in its early years. Three years later, in 1903, Jane Addams, Leonora O'Reilly, and other reformers founded the Women's Trade Union League (WTUL).

The WTUL was an organization dedicated to campaigning for working women and female suffrage. The first three leagues were established in

TURNING POINT

THE CHILDREN'S CRUSADE

One of the first examples of direct action took place in 1903, when radical labor campaigner Mother Jones organized child workers from clothing mills and mines in Pennsylvania to take part in a children's crusade. Led by Mother Jones, the children marched for 125 miles from Philadelphia to the New York home of President Theodore Roosevelt. Even though the president refused to meet the marchers, Mother Jones succeeded in turning the issue of child labor into a public scandal.

Left: Mary Harris Jones—known as "Mother Jones"—was a determined fighter for workers' rights. In 1902, she was put on trial for supporting a miners' strike and was described by the prosecuting lawyer as "the most dangerous woman in America."

Boston, Chicago, and New York with the motto "The Eight Hour Day, [and] a Living Wage to Guard the Home." Not all members of the WTUL were wage earners. A large proportion of the membership were wealthy, progressive women, who liked to be known as "allies," although their critics sometimes called them the "mink brigade" because of the fur coats they wore.

THE IWW

In 1905, the Industrial Workers of the World (IWW) was founded in Chicago. It was formed by militant unionists, socialists, anarchists, and other labor radicals. It aimed to organize all workers into "One Big Union," undivided by sex, race, or skills. Members of the IWW (often known as "Wobblies") urged direct action, such as strikes and picketing (standing in protest outside a place of work). Among its early women members were Mary Harris Jones (known as "Mother Jones"), who led the "Children's Crusade," and Elizabeth Gurley Flynn, who organized the mill workers' strike in Lawrence, Massachusetts.

FIGHTING IN THE COURTS

Sometimes the Progressives fought their battles in the law courts. In 1908, a famous case was heard between Curt Muller, the owner of a laundry business, and the State of Oregon. Muller had been forcing

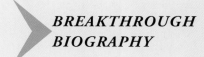

BREAKTHROUGH BIOGRAPHY

FLORENCE KELLEY (1859–1932)

Florence Kelley was born into a wealthy family in Philadelphia. After studying at Cornell University, she traveled to Europe and became a follower of communist thinkers Karl Marx and Friedrich Engels. She was a founding member of the settlement house movement and a passionate supporter of African-American suffrage, but is best known for her work on labor reform. Among her campaigns, Kelley fought to make it illegal to employ children under the age of fourteen. She also put pressure on employers to raise the minimum wage and cut working hours. She founded the National Consumers League and played a major part in the crucial case of *Muller v. Oregon.*

his female employees to work much longer than the state maximum of ten hours per day. Lawyer Florence Kelley and her friend Louis Brandeis (later a U.S. Supreme Court justice) won the case for the state of Oregon by arguing on medical grounds that long working hours had a harmful effect on women's health.

THE UPRISING OF 20,000

On November 22, 1909, one of the largest strikes in the history of the United States began in New York. Following weeks of unrest in the city's clothing factories, garment worker Clara Lemlich called for a general strike, triggering a massive walkout across the city. The next morning, more than 20,000 makers of shirtwaists (a type of woman's blouse) went on strike for better conditions and pay as laid down by the International Ladies' Garment Workers' Union.

Many employers responded with anger, using company guards to threaten picketers and calling in the police to arrest them. Within a month, more than 700 women strikers had been arrested and nineteen had been sentenced to spend time in the workhouse. However, the workers had powerful friends in the Progressive movement. Some of New York's wealthiest women paid the bail money to release the protesters and raised money to support the strikers and their families.

TURNING POINT

GARMENT WORKERS' STRIKES

The Uprising of 20,000 was the first in a series of strikes by clothing workers between the years 1909 and 1914. The strikes gained public support for the garment workers and built up the power of the ILGWU. This eventually led to improved conditions in the clothing industry across America.

Below: This photograph, taken in New York City in 1909, shows a group of striking textile workers from a shirtwaist factory.

By January, most of the small garment workshops had signed contracts with the ILGWU. The larger factories still refused to bargain with the union, but they did agree to some changes in hours and pay, and the strike eventually came to an end in February 1910.

THE TRIANGLE SHIRTWAIST FIRE

One of the firms that refused to sign a union contract was the Triangle Shirtwaist Company. Its owners ignored demands for safer working conditions, and following the strike, its workers returned to the same cramped and dangerous workrooms as before.

On March 25, 1911, a fire broke out in the Triangle factory. There was no sprinkler system, the fire escapes were inadequate, and the factory doors were bolted from the outside, probably to prevent the workers from taking unauthorized breaks. Some young women jumped from the windows to their death on the pavement below. Others died of burns or suffocation inside the building. That night, 146 corpses were laid out in the street and 2,000 people searched among the bodies for their relatives.

AFTER THE FIRE

The fire at the Triangle Shirtwaist factory sparked enormous public shock and outrage, and union members planned a dramatic protest. On April 5, 1911, they held a

DEATH TRAP

"Word had spread through the East Side, by some magic of terror, that the plant of the Triangle Waist Company was on fire and that several hundred workers were trapped. Horrified and helpless, the crowds—I among them—looked up at the burning building, saw girl after girl appear at the reddened windows, pause for a terrified moment, and then leap to the pavement below. . . . The emotions of the crowd were indescribable. Women were hysterical, scores fainted; men wept as, in paroxysms of frenzy, they hurled themselves against the police lines."

New York Assembly member Lewis Waldman, recalling the Triangle fire in his memoirs

Right: People watch as firefighters try to put out the fire at the Triangle Shirtwaist factory in New York City.

Above: Family members arrive at the New York City morgue (the place where dead bodies are kept before burial). They are checking the corpses to see if they can identify relatives and friends killed in the Triangle Shirtwaist fire.

TURNING POINT

FIRE PRECAUTIONS

The Triangle Shirtwaist fire of 1911 had the result of pushing the U.S. government into action. Following the scandal of the fire, the press led a campaign to expose dangerous working conditions in factories. This put pressure on the government to make changes to the law. In 1911, the Factory Commission, headed by Samuel Gompers, president of the American Federation of Labor, recommended legislation that required exit doors to open outward and prohibited the locking of these doors. Also in 1911, the New York Fire College was formed to train new firefighters, and in 1912, the Bureau of Fire Prevention was created.

solemn funeral parade with an empty hearse. Thousands of mourners marched behind the hearse, while half a million people lined the streets to pay their respects to the dead.

In a legal hearing following the fire, the owners of the Triangle Shirtwaist Company were found not guilty of manslaughter. However, public horror at the disaster prompted politicians to make some major changes in the law concerning safety at work.

STRIKES AND STRUGGLES

In the years following the Triangle Shirtwaist fire, there were many more strikes for workers' rights. One of the most famous protests took place in Lawrence, Massachusetts, in 1912, when 25,000 mill workers went on strike for safer conditions and better pay. The workers were supported by Elizabeth Gurley Flynn of the IWW, and their protest became national news when a woman picketer was shot dead by police. It was known as the Bread and Roses strike because one picketer carried a placard saying "We Want Bread, but Roses Too!"

Right: World War I posters urged women to help the war effort by joining the Women's Land Army of America and working on farms. More than 20,000 women from cities and towns traveled to rural America to take over work from men who had gone to fight in the war.

WAR WORK

In spring 1917, thousands of American men began to leave for Europe to fight in World War I. Even after the war ended in November 1918, many of them did not return home immediately. This left significant gaps in the labor market, which were mostly filled by women. As part of the war effort, women took on a wide range of jobs in factories, steel mills, farms, and mines and also worked on trains and streetcars.

Some problems arose at the end of the war when the men returned to their old jobs to find that the women who had taken their place did not want to give up their employment. In 1919, male unions in Cleveland protested the use of female streetcar conductors and succeeded in getting all the women removed from their posts. In Detroit, female conductors managed to keep their jobs, but no more women were hired.

WHITE-COLLAR WORK

By 1920, women in the United States were taking on more "white-collar" jobs. Many of them worked as secretaries and bookkeepers, while others became saleswomen in department stores. In 1919, Lena Madesin Phillips founded the National Federation of Business and Professional Women's Clubs (BPW) to represent the interests of white-collar women workers, and within a year, 26,000 women had joined. At the same time, Phillips launched her journal *Independent Woman* to reflect the views of a new kind of working woman.

TURNING POINT

THE WOMEN'S BUREAU

In 1920, the Women's Bureau of the Department of Labor was formed to collect information about women in the workforce and to safeguard good working conditions. The bureau had grown out of the Women in Industry Service Bureau, formed in 1918, to supervise female employment during World War I. The government's creation of a Woman's Bureau in 1920 reflected a new attitude to the importance of women in the workplace.

CHAPTER 4

WOMEN AT WAR

URING THE TWO YEARS THAT THE UNITED STATES WAS involved in World War I, life changed dramatically for many women. American women joined the military for the first time. Female nurses and doctors cared for the wounded, and women volunteers worked in mobile canteens, serving food to soldiers. A few brave female journalists followed the troops into battle to report on the conflict. On the home front, many women joined the workforce when American men went off to fight, and some took over jobs that had always been seen as "men's work."

WOMEN IN THE NAVY

By the beginning of 1917, it was clear that the U.S. Navy would soon be needed in the war with Germany, and many young Americans decided to join up. There were no women in the armed forces, but this situation did not last for long. On March 17, 1917, eighteen-year-old Loretta Walsh enlisted for four years' service in the U.S. Naval Reserve. Four days later, she was sworn in as the navy's first yeoman (F), so becoming the first female member of the U.S. military.

Altogether, more than 11,000 women became female yeomen, or "yeomanettes" as they were commonly known. They were entitled to receive the same benefits as men, including equal pay, but they did not serve on ships. Most of the yeomanettes worked as typists or telephone operators, while a few developed specialist skills, becoming radio operators, electricians, pharmacists, photographers, fingerprint experts, or camouflage designers.

A large number of yeomanettes were stationed in the Naval Reserve headquarters in Washington, D.C., while

Left: A recruiting poster for the U.S. Navy, featuring a female yeoman.

26

❝

YEOMAN (F)

"The process of joining up was simple and speedy: first, an interview by a chief clerk, and then a physical exam at the Naval Hospital, an oath of allegiance and, presto, one was a 'Yeoman (F),' signed up for four years!"

An extract from *I was a Yeoman (F)*, a memoir by Mrs. Henry F. Butler

Left: A group of female yeomen pose with a sailor from the U.S. Navy.

TURNING POINT

WOMEN JOIN THE FORCES

On March 19, 1917, the Navy Department authorized the enrollment of women in the Naval Reserve. In the following two years, nearly 13,000 women enlisted in the U.S. Navy, Marine Corps, and Coast Guard. Yet in spite of women's loyal service, no woman was allowed to stay in her post after the end of World War I. By July 1919, all female members of the armed forces had been discharged from duty. It was not until the United States entered World War II that women were once again permitted to enter the armed forces.

others served in naval stations, hospitals, shipyards, and munitions factories around the country. Yeomanettes were also taught to march and drill at public rallies and troop send-offs, and proved to be very effective recruiting officers.

MARINES AND COAST GUARDS

On August 13, 1918, Opha Mae Johnson became the first of 305 women to be accepted for duty in the Marine Corps Reserve. Like the yeomanettes, the majority of women marines worked at the marines' headquarters in order to release more men for active service, while some filled jobs at recruiting stations throughout the United States. A handful of women were employed by the U.S. Coast Guard service, including nineteen-year-old twins Genevieve and Lucille Baker, who were transferred from the Naval Coastal Defense Reserve to become the first uniformed women in the Coast Guard.

VOLUNTEERS AT THE FRONT

Some adventurous women were determined to take part in the action of World War I. Many volunteered for aid organizations, while others formed enterprising new groups of their own. Women washed and mended uniforms and worked in canteens, producing hot meals for the troops. They also handed out cigarettes and candy and generally tried

Above: During World War I, many women worked in munitions factories, producing weapons, bombs, and bullets to be used in the conflict.

THE BLESSED WHITE DRESS

"I shall never forget as long as I live the blessed white dress she had on the night she recited to us. We had not seen a white dress . . . in years. There we were with our gas masks at alert, all ready to go into the line, and there she was talking to us just like a girl from home. It sure was a great sight, you bet."

During World War I, actress Sarah Willmer traveled ten miles through a storm to give a poetry reading to the troops. A soldier who was present at the occasion is quoted in *Into the Breach: American Women Overseas in World War I.*

to keep up the men's morale. Army orders to keep women away from the battlefront proved difficult to enforce. One commander complained that women ignored all orders to leave the men in their care and kept reappearing at the front line after they had been sent to the rear.

ENTERTAINING THE TROOPS

Not all the women at the front acted as mothers to the troops. Soldiers were also visited by female entertainers, who distracted them from the horrors of war with song-and-dance routines, dramatic readings, and poetry recitals. The best known of these was American singer Elsie Janis, who started performing for British and French troops in 1914, inspiring devotion from her audiences. Elsie became known as the "sweetheart of the American forces."

MILITARY NURSES

By 1900, women had been working as military nurses for over one hundred years, but their status was only made official at the start of the

20th century. The U.S. Army Nurse Corps was founded in 1901 and the Navy Nurse Corps in 1908. In the early years of the 20th century, some nurses served abroad, but the real test came when the United States entered World War I. Within a few months, the navy had created five base hospital units in France, Scotland, and Ireland and also established special navy operating teams, including nurses, working close to the battle lines. Some teams were based on hospital ships off the French coast. Others were loaned to the army and worked behind the front line, far from any regular hospitals.

By the end of World War I, more than 1,550 American nurses had served in naval hospitals and other medical facilities at home and abroad. Some of them had faced great danger, and at least three army nurses were awarded the Distinguished Service Cross in recognition of their bravery.

THE RED CROSS

Not all American nurses worked for the armed forces. Some chose to join the American Red Cross, which had been founded by Clara Barton in 1881. During World War I, the Red Cross staffed

WOMEN OF COURAGE AND CONVICTION

FRANCES GULICK (1891–1936)

Frances Gulick was a volunteer social worker for the American Young Men's Christian Association (YMCA) in France. She was attached to an army unit, running a canteen that provided food for soldiers. Frances stayed at her post in the French town of Vernaise for over eighteen months and continued to operate her canteen even when the town was shelled and bombed. She was awarded a U.S. Army citation for valor and courage on the field of battle.

Below: Red Cross workers cared for men who had been sent home wounded. Some of the men they tended were sent off to war again. This postcard shows Red Cross workers based in Savannah, Georgia.

CANTEEN SERVICE, SAVANNAH CHAPTER, AMERICAN RED CROSS AT WORK.

Join the Red Cross
All you need is a Heart and a Dollar
RED CROSS CHRISTMAS ROLL CALL, DEC.16–23

Above: Recruitment posters for the Red Cross made a powerful appeal to American women.

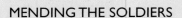

MENDING THE SOLDIERS

"Just as you send your clothes to the laundry and mend them when they come back, so we send our men to the trenches and mend them when they come back again."

Mary Borden, a Baltimore millionaire who ran an independent hospital unit at the front from 1914 to 1918

hospitals and ambulance companies in all the major battle zones. Red Cross nurses also played a major part in the care of victims of the worldwide influenza epidemic of 1918.

WOMEN DOCTORS

Before 1917, female doctors were not permitted to work in war zones. However, shortly after the United States joined the Allied forces in World War I, a committee was created by the Medical Women's National Association (later known as the American Medical Women's Association) to allow female physicians to provide care for the injured. Under the leadership of Dr. Rosalie Slaughter and Dr. Mary M. Crawford, the committee set about training an all-woman team of ambulance drivers, nurses, and physicians. This team worked in special hospitals close to the French battlefields, caring for wounded troops but also treating injured and sick civilians. After the war was over, many team members stayed on in Europe, offering medical care during the period of reconstruction.

FOREIGN CORRESPONDENTS

From the earliest days of World War I, American women reporters were stationed in Europe. When the Germans invaded Belgium in 1914, Mary Boyle O'Reilly, daughter of the publisher of *The Pilot*, a Catholic newspaper based in Boston, was on the spot and beat her male colleagues to report the story. In the following year, Mary Roberts Rinehart was sent by the *Saturday Evening Post* to cover the conflict in France and Belgium. Mary reported the German use of poison gas, but her editor declined to print her story, which was later written up by a male journalist.

In 1917, the U.S. government banned female reporters from the French and Belgian battlefields. This did not stop three resourceful women, Bessie Beatty of the *San Francisco Bulletin*, Louise Bryant of the *Bell Syndicate*, and Rheta Childe Dorr of the *New York Mail*, who all reported on the war from the Russian front.

USING LANGUAGE SKILLS

Apart from military nurses, the only American women to serve in the military overseas were members of the Army Signal Corps. A total of 223 women worked as telephone operators, linking the foot soldiers in the trenches to their generals behind the lines. The members of the signal corps were fluent in French and were known to the troops as the "hello girls."

ON THE HOME FRONT

Once the United States declared war on Germany, thousands of young men abandoned their jobs and joined the armed forces. It soon became clear that women would need to take men's place in the workforce. In the years 1917 to 1918, women took on a range of vital jobs. Some worked in munitions factories, producing weapons and ammunition to be used in the war.

CAMPAIGNING FOR PEACE

Not all American women supported the idea of war. Following the outbreak of World War I in Europe, a group of women pacifists in the United States

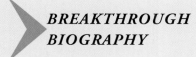

BREAKTHROUGH BIOGRAPHY

MARY ROBERTS RINEHART (1876–1958)

Mary grew up in Pittsburgh, where she trained to be a nurse, but she left nursing after she married a doctor. When she was twenty-seven, her husband lost all his savings, so she began writing to help support her family of three small children. Mary wrote stories, poems, and articles and even traveled to Europe to report on World War I. She continued writing all her life and is best known for her mystery stories.

Below: Mary Roberts Rinehart became very popular as a writer of mystery stories. She is often known as the "American Agatha Christie."

Right: Female pacifists campaigned against business speculators, who tried to make money out of World War I. In this photograph, women are marching in protest through New York City in 1916.

TURNING POINT

VOTING RIGHTS

The vital part played by women in World War I persuaded President Woodrow Wilson that he should back a federal amendment supporting women's voting rights. In September 1918, he urged the Senate to pass the amendment and appealed to the senators to recognize the contributions made by American women in the war:

"We have made partners of the women in this war; shall we admit them only to a partnership of suffering and sacrifice and toil and not to a partnership of privilege and right?"

decided to form an organization to help put an end to the conflict. They felt frustrated by the lack of progress made by male pacifist groups and maintained that women were in a better position to put pressure on governments because of their role as "custodians of life."

THE WOMEN'S PEACE PARTY

On January 10, 1915, over 3,000 women attended a meeting in the ballroom of the New Willard Hotel in Washington and formed the Woman's Peace Party (also known as the WPP). Jane Addams was elected chairman, and the committee was made up of many prominent figures in the Progressive movement, including Florence Kelley, Anna Howard Shaw, Lillian Wald, and Carrie Chapman Catt.

With the support of the international women's peace movement, the WPP aimed to persuade President Woodrow Wilson to act as mediator between opposing countries rather than joining the conflict. But they faced opposition from many critics, who attacked them in the press as "hysterical pacifists." Despite these criticisms, the WPP continued to grow and by 1917 had attracted 40,000 members.

AFTER 1917

After the United States entered the war, the peace movement fragmented. The leaders of the WPP made the decision to put aside their public opposition to the war and concentrate instead on making plans for the post-war period. In 1919, the Women's Peace Conference was held in Switzerland, and women from sixteen countries agreed that the WPP would become part of the Women's International League for Peace and Freedom (WILFPF).

Below: On August 29, 1914, members of the Women's Peace Party (WPP) march through the streets of New York City, watched by large crowds.

WAR AND PEACE

"We women of the United States, assembled in behalf of World Peace, grateful for the security of our own country, but sorrowing for the misery of all involved in the present struggle among warring nations, do hereby band ourselves together to demand that war be abolished. As women, we are particularly charged with the future of childhood and with the care of the helpless and the unfortunate. . . . We demand that women be given a share in deciding between war and peace in all the courts of high debate—within the home, the school, the church, the industrial order and the state."

A statement issued by the Women's Peace Party, January 10, 1915

CHAPTER 5

WINNING THE VOTE

IN THE OPENING YEARS OF THE 20TH CENTURY, THE CAMPAIGN to win voting rights for women seemed to have run out of steam, but within ten years, it had gained new energy. During this period, campaigners split into two main groups, each of which used different methods in their attempt to achieve women's suffrage (the right to vote in elections). Thanks to the efforts of some remarkable women, the campaigners achieved their objective in 1920. On August 26, the 19th Amendment to the U.S. Constitution was passed, granting all women the right to vote.

TIME FOR CHANGE

The women's suffrage movement had begun in the 1840s under the leadership of such inspiring figures as Susan B. Anthony and Sojourner Truth. However, by the end of the 19th century, most of the early

WOMEN OF COURAGE AND CONVICTION

CARRIE CHAPMAN CATT (1859–1947)

Carrie Chapman Catt became involved in the women's suffrage movement in the 1880s and was made president of NAWSA at age forty-one. Catt served as president from 1900 to 1904 and again from 1915 to 1920. She devoted herself to the movement, leading dozens of campaigns, making hundreds of speeches, and mobilizing over a million volunteers. She was also active in the international suffrage movement, the Women's Peace Party, and the Women's Christian Temperance Movement.

Right: Carrie Chapman Catt was admired for her clever use of tactics in gaining support for female suffrage.

Left: The official program of a women's suffrage rally, held in Washington, D.C., in 1913. The female campaigners are deliberately portrayed as courageous knights on a heroic quest.

leaders were either dead or no longer actively campaigning. In 1900, Susan B. Anthony resigned as president of the National American Woman Suffrage Association (NAWSA), leaving Carrie Chapman Catt in charge of an organization that was very low on funds.

As the new president of NAWSA, Catt faced some daunting challenges. By 1900, women had gained the right to vote in only four western states (Wyoming, Utah, Colorado, and Idaho), and it seemed unlikely they would do so in any other states. The NAWSA members were scattered, inactive, and discouraged. To add to Catt's problems, there was a powerful anti-suffrage movement that opposed any change in society as dangerous, unnatural, and even sinful for breaking God's law.

CATT'S "SOCIETY PLAN"

Fortunately, Catt rose to the challenge. Recognizing that suffragettes were generally seen as dangerous outsiders, she devised a "society plan" to give her movement a new image of respectability. In the early years of the 20th century, she set about recruiting "society women" from wealthy families all over America. By gaining the support of these powerful women, she made NAWSA respectable and gained the financial backing she needed.

A NEW CLASS OF SISTER

"*The spectacle was most impressive. It was not only that there were so many women, but the character of representation was formidable. The shrieking sisterhood of the old days was in the minority. There were wives of men of large importance in the community, bankers, merchants and lawyers. There were women of the best lineage whose influence is in most circumstances exerted only for the good. . . . [But] these women are in the wrong. . . . They are bringing their good names to the support of a movement that is unreasonable, revolutionary and opposed to their best interests.*"

An article from the *New York Times* about a suffrage rally held in 1909. The report recognizes the impressive character of the women protesters but condemns their cause as wrong.

Right: The women's suffrage movement faced determined opposition from anti-suffragists, who claimed that women were deserting their proper roles as wives and mothers. Posters like this, showing downtrodden husbands and family misery, were used by the anti-suffragists to try to turn the public against the women's movement.

Once she had secured support and funds, Catt concentrated on campaigning at the state level. NAWSA directed most of its resources into a few key campaigns, where there was a strong chance of winning. This approach paid off in 1910 when Washington State granted women the right to vote; California followed suit in 1911. Over the next five years, suffrage was also secured in Arizona, Kansas, Oregon, Montana, Nevada, Illinois, and Alaska.

SPLITTING AWAY

In 1905, Carrie Chapman Catt resigned as president of NAWSA to care for her husband, who was seriously ill, and was replaced by the less dynamic Dr. Anna Howard Shaw. At the same time, some members of the suffrage movement were becoming impatient with

NAWSA's approach. Women such as Alice Paul, Lucy Burns, Harriot Stanton Blatch, and Alice Stone Blackwell wanted to try more militant methods and began to form breakaway groups.

MILITANT METHODS

The most successful new group was the Congressional Union for Woman Suffrage (CUWS). Created in 1913 by Alice Paul and Lucy Burns, it was later reorganized as the National Woman's Party (NWP) in 1916. By 1914, the CUWS had a membership of 4,500 and had raised more than $50,000 for its campaign. It also had its own magazine, *The Suffragist*, filled with radical articles and cartoons and edited by courageous journalist Rheta Childe Dorr.

Following the example of the British suffragettes, members of the CUWS held large demonstrations, parades, and motorcades and organized public debates on street corners. They recruited working-class women to their cause, combining demands for suffrage with campaigns for workers' rights.

ANTI-SUFFRAGISTS

The militant methods adopted by the CUWS resulted in a surge of anti-suffragist feeling. The anti-suffragist movement consisted of men and women who believed a woman's proper place was in the home. Anti-suffragists claimed that if women were allowed to vote, American family life would be threatened.

The majority of anti-suffragists merely expressed negative opinions about the suffrage movement, but a few joined official associations. The New York State Association Opposed to Woman Suffrage was founded in 1897. In

Right: Harriot Stanton Blatch, shown here pinning up a pro-suffrage poster, was a leading figure in the campaign for votes for women.

Above: The "silent sentinels" stood in protest outside the White House, holding up their placards so they could be seen by President Woodrow Wilson every time he looked out of the window.

1908, it had over ninety members active in producing pamphlets and publications explaining its views.

A "WINNING PLAN"

In 1915, Carrie Chapman Catt once again became president of NAWSA and soon announced her "winning plan" to push a suffrage bill through the Senate. Catt worked hard to achieve this aim by gently pressuring senators and congressmen and by persuading the president himself. As part of her campaign, she urged all her supporters to "keep the suffrage noise up" around the country.

SILENT SENTINELS

While NAWSA members followed Carrie Chapman Catt's plan, the leaders of the National Woman's Party adopted more radical tactics. In January 1917, Alice Paul and Lucy Burns led the National Woman's Party in a daring campaign. It involved women protesters standing outside the White House in a silent, nonstop vigil. The protesters held placards demanding equal rights for women and vowed not to leave until President Woodrow Wilson had agreed to give his support to women's suffrage.

At first, the president ignored the "silent sentinels," but in June 1917, police began to arrest protesters on the charge of obstructing the traffic. Many of the women were sent to prison, and some went on hunger strikes in protest against the conditions there. In a few cases, women were tortured and beaten, and when reports reached the newspapers about their treatment, there was a public outcry. In November 1917, all the women were released, and in March 1918, a judge declared that the arrests, trials, and imprisonments had all been illegal. By then, President Wilson had been converted to the suffrage cause and had urged the Senate to give their support to voting rights for women.

WORLD WAR I AND THE SUFFRAGISTS

After the United States entered World War I in April 1917, the different branches of the suffragist movement responded in contrasting ways to the new situation. Under the leadership of Carrie Chapman Catt, NAWSA members followed a patriotic line. Campaigners ceased to criticize the president and adopted a much more low-key approach in their campaigns. By contrast, the National Woman's Party, led by Alice Paul, remained as determined as ever in its protests.

The silent sentinel campaign was not interrupted, and protesters continued to carry placards attacking the president. This had the effect of turning many members of the public against them, and some of the "sentinels" were assaulted both verbally and physically because of their alleged lack of patriotism. However, as the months wore on and the sentinels suffered increasingly harsh treatment, many people changed their minds and began to support the women's cause.

THE PRESSURE MOUNTS

By the beginning of 1918, pressure was mounting on President Woodrow Wilson to take action on women's suffrage. Public sympathy

TURNING POINT

NEW YORK PARADE

On October 27, 1918, the women's suffrage movement held its annual parade in New York. By this time, the United States had been at war for eighteen months. The protesters were joined by women in uniform, including a number of Red Cross nurses. The presence of these courageous women who had served their country helped to tip public opinion in favor of women's rights.

Below: Women carry ballot boxes on a stretcher at a suffrage parade in New York City in 1915. There were numerous suffrage protests in the years leading up to World War I.

WOMEN OF COURAGE AND CONVICTION

ALICE PAUL (1885–1977)

Alice Paul grew up as a Quaker in New Jersey and studied political science in the United States and Britain. In 1913, she created the CUWS with her friend Lucy Burns. This soon developed into the National Woman's Party, the most radical branch of the women's suffrage movement. Paul employed a range of militant methods, but her most famous campaign was the silent sentinels' vigil outside the White House. In July 1917, she was arrested, along with other sentinels, and imprisoned. When she began a hunger strike in protest at the conditions, she was moved to a psychiatric prison ward and force-fed raw eggs through a tube. Paul's determination and sufferings helped to change public opinion about the justice of her cause.

had moved toward support of the silent sentinels, and Carrie Chapman Catt had been busy behind the scenes pursuing her highly effective campaign of persuasion. In addition, there was a growing public belief that the women who served their country in the war deserved to be granted equal rights with men.

THE 19TH AMENDMENT

On January 10, 1918, a suffrage bill was brought before the House of Representatives. The bill proposed an amendment to the U.S. Constitution that would grant voting rights to all American women. On the previous evening, President

Below: As women wave and cheer, Alice Paul stands on a balcony and unfurls a banner celebrating the state of Tennessee's ratification of (giving formal consent to) the 19th Amendment, granting women the right to vote.

Wilson had made a widely published appeal to members of the House of Representatives recommending that they pass the bill and stressing its importance as a war measure. The bill was passed by a margin of one vote and brought to the Senate.

On September 30, 1918, President Wilson appealed to the Senate to pass the suffrage bill, speaking passionately about the contribution that American women had made to the war effort. But despite the president's efforts, two votes were lacking to gain the majority needed to pass the bill. It took a determined nationwide campaign by suffragists to secure sufficient support for the bill, but on June 4, 1919, the Senate eventually gave its approval. The 19th Amendment to the Constitution became law on August 26, 1920. Three months later, a presidential election was held, and for the first time, women in all states had the right to vote.

TURNING POINT

VOTES FOR WOMEN

The suffrage movement in the United States was part of a worldwide campaign to gain votes for women. The first nation to grant full suffrage to women was New Zealand, in 1893. Over the next twenty years, most of the Scandinavian nations and Australia followed New Zealand's example. Canada and the United Kingdom granted women the vote in 1918, although in the United Kingdom, only women over age thirty were allowed to vote.

AFTER THE AMENDMENT

Once the suffrage movement had achieved its aims, a different kind of organization was needed. The National League of Women Voters (NLWV) was established in 1920 to educate women about their rights, study national social policy, and take part in local politics. The NLVW also sponsored Women's Equality Day, held on August 26 to celebrate the anniversary of the 19th Amendment. However, the battle for universal suffrage was not yet won. Many African-American women still faced obstacles when they went to vote, and some courageous women championed their cause.

Right: In November 1920, women all over the United States went to the polling booths for the first time to cast their votes in a presidential election.

CHAPTER 6

ACHIEVEMENTS

I N THE OPENING DECADES OF THE 20TH CENTURY, some adventurous women began to break free of their traditional roles as wives and mothers. Opportunities for education increased, and more women chose to pursue careers in business, science, and politics. Women competed with men in literature and the arts, and in the early 20th century, inspiring female stars emerged in show business, music, and theater.

EDUCATION

Opportunities for education increased rapidly in the opening years of the 20th century. In 1900, just thirty-one states required children between age eight and fourteen to attend school, but ten years later, 72 percent of American children were attending elementary school. For the privileged few, there was also the chance to go to college. Female college enrollment tripled in the period between 1890 and 1910.

SPORTS

In the early 20th century, female baseball and hockey teams were formed. American women also began to compete seriously in the fields of swimming, tennis, and figure skating, winning international prizes. Two major tennis champions were May Sutton and Hazel Wightman. In 1905, Sutton won the women's

Left: A poster in the fashionable art nouveau style showing a female student in a library.

Above: May Sutton was only eighteen years old when she first won the women's singles title at the U.S. National Championships in 1904.

singles title at Wimbledon and at the U.S. Lawn Tennis Association (USTLA). During her career, Wightman won a total of twelve USTLA singles and doubles titles. She later created the Wightman Cup for women tennis players as a counterpart to the Davis Cup for men.

SCIENCE

Women helped to achieve some important scientific breakthroughs in the early 20th century. For example, medical researcher Maud Slye advanced the understanding of cancer through her studies of mice. Another outstanding researcher, Nettie Stevens, worked in the field of

BREAKTHROUGH BIOGRAPHY

NETTIE MARIA STEVENS (1861–1912)

Nettie Maria Stevens was the daughter of a carpenter. She worked as a schoolteacher and librarian before enrolling at Stanford University at the age of thirty-five. For the next four years, Stevens studied physiology and biology at Stanford. Then she moved to Bryn Mawr College in Pennsylvania to work on a doctorate. Stevens proved to be such an exceptional student that she was awarded a fellowship to study in Italy and Germany. In 1903, she completed her PhD (doctorate) and began a research job in the relatively new field of genetics. Stevens worked in the genetics laboratory at Bryn Mawr until her death at age fifty-one.

TURNING POINT

WOMEN IN THE OLYMPICS

The 1900 Olympic Games, held in Paris, France, marked a significant milestone in women's sports. For the first time in the history of the games, female athletes were permitted to compete in Olympic events. Just three sports admitted female contestants—tennis, golf, and croquet. American women were delighted when golfer Margaret Abbott won a gold medal for the United States.

genetics and discovered the chromosomes that determine an individual's gender. At this time, women scientists were not always taken seriously, so Stevens's discovery was widely credited to her male colleague Edmund Wilson.

In the field of astronomy, Henrietta Leavitt worked at the Harvard College Observatory as a "human computer," counting images on photographic plates. By studying these plates, she discovered a kind of pulsating star. This was a breakthrough that changed the nature of modern astronomy, but Leavitt received almost no recognition for her achievement.

Below: A poster for the extremely popular Ziegfeld Follies. Many female stars launched their show business careers by singing or dancing in the Follies.

ZIEGFELD DANSE DE FOLLIES
Atop New Amsterdam Theatre

ZIEGFELD 9 O'CLOCK REVUE & ZIEGFELD MID NIGHT FROLIC

SHOW BUSINESS

At the beginning of the 20th century, vaudeville shows were the most popular form of public entertainment. They included song-and-dance and comedy routines and were enjoyed by both men and women. One of the most famous vaudeville shows was the Ziegfeld Follies, which first appeared on Broadway in 1907 and featured such female stars as Nora Bayes, Fanny Brice, and Eva Tanguay. Bayes was famous for the song "Shine on Harvest Moon," which she wrote with her husband, Jack Norwood. Brice was a comedian whose life was later dramatized in the film *Funny Girl*, and Tanguay was an all-around performer who shocked and delighted audiences with her revealing costumes.

THEATER

Theater flourished at the turn of the century, providing a showcase for the talents of female writers, producers, and actors. Beginning in 1906, playwright Rachel Crothers wrote, directed, and produced one play a year for thirty years. Another female director, Jessie Bonstelle, had a massive hit with her production of Louisa May Alcott's *Little Women*.

Above: Maude Adams in the Peter Pan costume that she designed herself. "Maudie," as she was popularly known, was the highest-paid performer of her day, with a yearly income of more than $1 million during the 1900s.

Theater was an excellent vehicle for new ideas about women. In 1909, actress Mary Shaw starred in Elizabeth Robins's suffrage play *Votes for Women.* Four years earlier, she had played the lead in George Bernard Shaw's *Mrs. Warren's Profession,* a play about prostitution, which was shut down on grounds of "indecency." Not all plays were intended to educate their audiences. A smash hit of the period was J. M. Barrie's *Peter Pan,* starring Maude Adams in the title role. Adams also designed her own costume, including a round collar that became known as a "Peter Pan" collar.

MOVIES

The movie business took off in the second decade of the 20th century. Soon there were picture houses all over America, showing silent films with piano accompaniments. Early stars of the silent screen included

BREAKTHROUGH BIOGRAPHY

MARY PICKFORD (1892–1979)

Mary Pickford was born and brought up in Canada. She worked as a touring actress before landing a small part in a Broadway play. In 1909, she was given a screen test by the Biograph Company, which employed her in Hollywood to act in over fifty short movies. By 1912, Pickford was starring in longer films and had become a major box office attraction. Her hits included *The Poor Little Rich Girl* (1917), *Rebecca of Sunnybrook Farm* (1917), and *Pollyanna* (1920). After the arrival of sound movies in 1929, her popularity fell sharply. In 1919, she co-founded the company United Artists with movie director D. W. Griffith, actor and director Charlie Chaplin, and the second of her three husbands, actor Douglas Fairbanks.

Above: Journalist Ida Tarbell was fearless in her exposure of corrupt business practices. She is shown here leaving the house of a striker who had been killed during a workers' protest in Roosevelt, New Jersey, in 1915.

Mary Pickford, Theda Bara, and sisters Dorothy and Lilian Gish. Stuntwoman Pearl White was a sensation in a series of "cliff-hanger" films, and screenwriter Anita Loos composed over 100 scripts, mainly for silent movies.

JOURNALISTS

Women began to make their mark as journalists in the early years of the 20th century. Many wrote on traditionally feminine topics, such as fashion and cooking, but others worked as foreign correspondents and investigative reporters. Female foreign correspondents traveled to dangerous parts of the world, even reporting from war zones, while fearless investigative journalists exposed corruption and injustice. Two of the latter were Ida M. Tarbell and Rheta Childe Dorr. Tarbell made her name with a nineteen-part series in *McClure's Magazine*, exposing the corrupt practices within John D. Rockefeller's Standard Oil Company. Her thorough and fearless exposure managed to bring down one of the world's most powerful men and break his company's stranglehold on the oil industry.

THE MARRIAGE TRAP

"The trouble is you . . . have to marry a man before you can find out the sort of wife he needs; and usually it's exactly the sort you are not."

An extract from *O Pioneers!*, published in 1913, Willa Cather's novel about the harsh lives of frontier farmers on the American prairies

Left: Willa Cather had a hard childhood, growing up on a farm in Nebraska as the oldest of seven children. Most of her novels reflect her childhood experiences.

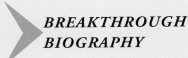

BREAKTHROUGH BIOGRAPHY

EDNA ST. VINCENT MILLAY (1892–1950)

Edna St. Vincent Millay (known to her friends as "Vincent") grew up in Maine. Her mother raised her daughters alone and encouraged them to be ambitious and self-reliant. Millay's poetic talent was recognized at the age of twenty when she entered a national poetry contest. She later won a scholarship to Vassar women's college. After leaving Vassar, Millay lived in Greenwich Village, New York, before marrying and moving to a farmhouse in upstate New York. She had several passionate relationships with both women and men. Many people were shocked by the frank expression of female sexuality in some of her poems.

NOVELISTS

Some outstanding women writers emerged in the period 1900 to 1920. In 1905, Edith Wharton wrote *The House of Mirth*, the first of a series of novels about high-society life in New York. Sixteen years later, she won the Pulitzer Prize for *The Age of Innocence*, becoming the first woman to receive the award. Willa Cather also won the Pulitzer Prize in 1923, but her novels present a picture of a very different America. She grew up in Nebraska and is best known for her description of frontier life on the prairies in novels such as *O Pioneers!* and *My Antonia*. Other female writers of the period include Kate Douglas Wiggin, who wrote the classic children's story *Rebecca of Sunnybrook Farm*, and Gertrude Stein, who experimented with new forms of writing. Stein's first book, *Three Lives*, published in 1909, tells the story of three working-class women.

POETS

Edna St. Vincent Millay and Amy Lowell both won the Pulitzer Prize for Poetry (in 1923 and 1926 respectively). Millay had gained instant fame in 1912 when she entered her poem "Renascence" in a contest

BREAKTHROUGH BIOGRAPHY

FLORENCE ELLINWOOD ALLEN (1884–1966)

Florence Ellinwood Allen grew up in Cleveland, Ohio. She began studying to be a concert pianist, but an injury led to a change of career, and in 1906 she started work as a music critic. During this time, Allen developed an interest in politics and law. As a university student, she studied those subjects, qualifying as a lawyer at the age of thirty. Gradually her legal career flourished, and in 1920 she was made an appeals court judge. Two years later, she was appointed as an Ohio State Supreme Court judge. In addition to being a greatly respected judge, Wells encouraged young women to train as lawyers and was a passionate supporter of the suffrage and pacifist movements.

in *The Lyric Year*. It was widely considered to be the best entry, and when it was placed fourth, there was a public outcry. Amy Lowell started to publish poetry in 1912 and was immediately recognized as an outstanding new talent. One of her most famous poems, "Patterns," is a powerful anti-war statement.

BUSINESSWOMEN

One of the most outstanding businesswomen of the period was Rose Markward Knox. In 1896, she and her husband set up a factory to make gelatin, and when he died in 1908, Rose took over the job of running the business, introducing several changes of her own. Her first was to lock the back door of the factory, which had been used as an entrance for the women workers. Knox said that men and women were equal, so they should all enter by the front door. Over the next few years, Knox made several changes to ensure that her workers were well treated. These included giving her employees two weeks' paid vacation, something almost unheard of until that point. In 1925, after seventeen years under Rose's leadership, the Knox Gelatin Company was worth $1 million.

Another successful businesswoman was Lena Himmelstein, also known as Lane Bryant, whose clothing store for pregnant and larger women proved so successful that she established a chain of Lane Bryant stores. Like Rose Knox, she took the trouble to look after her employees, offering them profit-sharing options, pensions, life insurance plans, and medical benefits.

NEW CAREERS

Several women made exciting career breakthroughs in the early years of the 20th century. In 1910, Alice Stebbins Wells joined

Left: Helena Rubinstein was born in Poland and emigrated to Australia as a child. Following the outbreak of World War I, she moved to New York City, where she opened a cosmetics salon in 1915. From this simple start, Rubinstein built a multimillion-dollar beauty business.

the Los Angeles police force as America's first female police officer. Within five years, sixteen cities had hired women officers and Wells had formed the International Association of Policewomen.

In 1911, Emma Jentzer was employed as the first female special agent in the Bureau of Investigations (later the Federal Bureau of Investigation, or FBI). In 1920, Florence Ellinwood Allen was the first woman to be appointed as an appeals court judge, beating nine male candidates out for the job. In the field of politics, Jeannette Rankin, a Republican from Montana, was elected to the House of Representatives on November 7, 1916, becoming the first woman to serve in Congress.

Below: Early members of the American Girl Scouts with Juliette Low, their founder, on the far right. Low recognized that the Scouting movement could give girls a sense of independence and adventure that would equip them for significant achievements in later life.

TURNING POINT

THE GIRL SCOUTS OF AMERICA

On March 12, 1912, Juliette Gordon Low gathered eighteen girls in Savannah, Georgia, to register the first troop of American Girl Scouts. Low had been inspired by the Scouting movement while she was in Britain, and when she returned to the United States, she was determined to set up an organization for American girls. Before the meeting, she made a historic telephone call to her cousin: "Come right over! I've got something for the girls of Savannah, and all of America, and all the world, and we're going to start it tonight!"

CHAPTER 7

MINORITY GROUPS

I N THE EARLY 20TH CENTURY, LIFE WAS VERY HARD for many women in America. African Americans, recent immigrants, Native Americans, members of minority religious groups, and disabled women all suffered discrimination, injustice, and even ill treatment. In response to these problems, women began to organize societies to care for members of their community and campaign for equal rights.

Above: African Americans were usually given the worst-paid jobs in any community. This photograph shows female street sweepers in Belton, South Carolina, in 1905.

AN EQUAL CHANCE

""And so lifting as we climb, onward and upward we go, struggling and striving. . . . Seeking no favors because of our color or patronage because of our needs, we knock at the bar of justice and ask for an equal chance."

An extract from a speech by Mary Church Terrell on the aims and work of the National Association of Colored Women

THE BLACK WOMEN'S CLUB MOVEMENT

African-American men and women faced open discrimination in the early years of the 20th century. Public transportation, medical facilities, and social meeting places were commonly segregated with different areas for "blacks" and "whites." In the workplace, African

Americans were not admitted into trade unions and so had no protection against unfair treatment. In addition to all these disadvantages, black American women faced discrimination because of their gender.

In the closing years of the 19th century, some black women decided to form their own organizations to fight for better treatment and to deal with social welfare issues within their communities. One of the earliest of these black women's clubs was the National Association of Colored Women (NACW), founded in 1896. By the early 1900s, NACW had branches all over the United States led by educated, middle-class black women. The first objective of the clubs was to improve the lives of the poorer and more vulnerable members of their communities. In addition to providing health care and food for the poor, they financed schools, orphanages, homes for older people, and shelters for young women (all of which were generally provided for whites by the local government).

FIGHTING FOR RIGHTS

The black women's clubs were not just social welfare organizations. Club members also organized civil rights actions and voter registration and education. They focused on programs that stressed racial pride and the improvement of conditions for blacks. In particular, NACW members worked to reduce the risks of sexual exploitation and abuse associated with the work of live-in domestics, the largest employment category for black women at the turn of the century.

VOTING RIGHTS

Many African Americans joined the women's suffrage movement, but they were not always treated well by white campaigners. In the southern states, some white suffragists did not believe that black women should have the right to vote. A low point was reached in 1913 at a

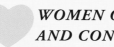

WOMEN OF COURAGE AND CONVICTION

MARY CHURCH TERRELL (1863–1954)

Mary Church Terrell was the daughter of two former slaves. Her father built up a real estate business, earning enough money to send Mary to Oberlin College in Ohio, where she earned both bachelor's and master's degrees. Terrell became a high-school teacher, rising to the position of principal. In 1896, she became the first president of NACW and led the movement until 1900. In addition to her work for the NACW, Terrell played an important role in the campaign for women's suffrage. In the last years of her life, she led a successful battle in Washington, D.C., against segregation in public eating places.

Below: Mary Church Terrell represented women of color on the American delegation to the International Congress of Women in Berlin in 1904.

Above: At the suffrage parade through Washington, D.C., in 1913, some southern suffragists refused to march with their black sisters. The leaders of the suffrage movement faced criticism from some of their members because they failed to take a firm stand against racism.

suffrage parade in Washington, D.C., when black participants were instructed to march at the rear. Refusing to do so, Ida Wells-Barnett joined the white protesters and was welcomed by some of the women.

Even after the 19th Amendment was passed granting all women the right to vote, black women faced obstacles in many states. Voting officials discouraged them by making them wait hours in line, imposing unfair tax and property requirements, and testing their education before they could register to vote.

WHITE SUPPORT

In 1909, black and white Americans joined to form the National Association for the Advancement of Colored People (NAACP). Women played a prominent part in the association. Among its active members were Mary White Ovington, Jane Addams, Florence Kelley, and Lillian Wald, who worked alongside black women leaders such as Mary Terrell and Ida Wells-Barnett.

WOMEN OF COURAGE AND CONVICTION

IDA WELLS-BARNETT (1862–1931)

Ida Wells-Barnett was a key figure in the struggle for rights for black women. She lived in Memphis, Tennessee, at a time when racial tensions were high and there were frequent lynchings (illegal hangings) of black men. Wells-Barnett led a national anti-lynching movement and campaigned for the protection of female domestic workers. She was an avid supporter of the women's suffrage movement. In 1913, she founded the Alpha Suffrage Club to campaign for voting rights for black women. She also edited a newspaper, the *Alpha Suffrage Record*.

Right: Ida Wells-Barnett reached a wide audience through her work as a radical journalist, a newspaper editor, and an inspiring leader in the civil rights movement.

PROBLEMS IN THE WORKPLACE

Black women faced great difficulties in the labor market. While African Americans had worked for generations in low-paid agricultural and domestic jobs, they struggled to gain better-paid and higher-profile jobs. This issue became a subject of widespread debate in 1903 when Minnie Cox, a black postmistress in Indianola, Mississippi, was forced to resign from her job by white racists. President Theodore Roosevelt refused to accept her resignation and instead suspended the postal service to Indianola, drawing national attention to the scandal.

Organizations such as the NAACP battled to gain better conditions and acceptance for black Americans in the workplace, and a few outstanding individuals, such as Madam C. J. Walker, built successful careers against enormous odds.

MUSICAL STARS

Several black women achieved success as musical stars in the early years of the 20th century. By the end of the 19th century, two forms of black music—ragtime and blues—began to reach wider audiences and became hugely popular. One of the best-known female ragtime stars was singer and dancer Aida Overton Walker, who played the lead in the all-black ragtime musical *In Dahomey*. In 1920, Mamie Smith cut the

BREAKTHROUGH BIOGRAPHY

MADAM C. J. WALKER (1867–1919)

Sarah Breedlove McWilliams (Madam C. J. Walker) was the daughter of two former slaves. She married at fourteen and was a widow by age twenty. Walker worked as a laundress to support her daughter and then became a sales agent for a hair-care company. In 1906, she married Charles Joseph Walker, changed her name to Madam C. J. Walker, and founded a company to sell hair-care products and cosmetics to black women. By 1917, Walker had become America's first self-made woman millionaire, and her company employed thousands of black women as sales agents.

Above: African-American blues star Mamie Smith, accompanied by her "Jazz Hounds" in New York City in 1920.

record *Crazy Blues*, the first successful recording of vocal blues by an African-American singer. The record was a huge hit, selling almost a million copies in one year.

HELPING IMMIGRANTS

There was a huge surge in immigration to the United States at the end of the 19th century. Most of the immigrants came from eastern and southern Europe and were bewildered by the unfamiliar culture they found in America. Immigrants usually ended up in the poorest districts of American cities, where they encountered discrimination and even violence. In response to these problems, some progressive women decided to form the Immigrants Protective League (IPL).

In 1908, the IPL was founded in Chicago by a group including Jane Addams and Grace Abbott. Under their leadership, the league established waiting rooms at railroad stations, where recent arrivals were given help finding relatives and friends. IPL members ran education programs, teaching language skills and housekeeping along with American values, ideas, and beliefs. Most of the league's efforts were directed at female immigrants, in the belief that women would pass on the American values they learned to their husbands and children.

JEWISH WOMEN

Jewish immigrants faced discrimination in their social lives and in the workplace. Many Jewish women were employed in the textile industry, where they had to work punishing hours doing backbreaking work. Rose Schneiderman worked in a New York factory and was horrified by the conditions. In 1903, she formed the Jewish Socialist United Cloth Hat and Cap Makers' Union to demand better treatment for textile workers.

Many Americans were unaware of the harsh conditions of immigrants' lives. Jewish novelist Anzia Yezierska helped gain public sympathy for Jews and Puerto Ricans through her stories of life on New York's Lower East Side. One of Yezierska's most successful works was *Bread Givers*, which tells the story of Sara and her Jewish immigrant family in New York.

NATIVE AMERICANS

By the early 20th century, life was grim for most Native Americans. Stripped of their native lands, most of them lived on reservations with little provision for education or health care. The reservations were far away from major towns, and there were few opportunities for employment, especially for women. In 1911, a group of educated Native Americans established the Society of American Indians. This organization put pressure on the government to provide more

---

Right: Rose Schneiderman represented women in the United States but also on the international stage. She is shown here (left) with colleague Mary Anderson on her way to the Paris Peace Conference in 1919.

WOMEN OF COURAGE AND CONVICTION

ROSE SCHNEIDERMAN (1882–1972)

Rose Schneiderman was born in Poland, but her family moved to New York when she was eight years old. Two years later, her father died and Rose was placed in an orphanage because her mother could not afford to keep her. She started work in a cap factory at age thirteen. After forming the Jewish Socialist United Cloth Hat and Cap Makers' Union, she led a successful thirteen-week cap makers' strike in New York in 1905. Rose soon became one of the leading members of the Women's Trade Union League. She played an active part in the shirtwaist workers' strike of 1909.

support for Native Americans, including improved health care and special law courts.

Some Native American women made determined efforts to promote their culture and encourage pride in their heritage. Nampeyo was a potter from the Hopi tribe who became famous for her traditional Pueblo ware. Angel De Cora of the Winnebago tribe was a talented artist whose paintings illustrated her childhood life on the Nebraska plains. She taught art to Native Americans and encouraged her students to use traditional designs in their work. Zitkala-Sa belonged to the Sioux tribe. She translated traditional Sioux stories into English in her book *Old Indian Legends*.

HISPANIC WOMEN

For most Hispanic people living in the southwestern United States, life was hard. Many families lived in poverty, and standards of education were low. Discrimination sometimes tipped over into violence, and Hispanic women were frequently exploited by their employers. Faced

> ## BREAKTHROUGH BIOGRAPHY
>
> ### NAMPEYO (1860?–1942)
>
> Nampeyo belonged to the Hopi people of the southwestern United States and lived on a reservation in Arizona. In the 1870s, she started making pots for the tourist market but then decided to return to more traditional forms and patterns. With the help of an archaeologist, Nampeyo collected fragments of ancient pots, which she used as the starting point for her designs. Her work was purchased by museums and collectors around the world. Nampeyo began to lose her sight in 1925, but she continued making pots by touch alone. She worked as a potter right up until her death.
>
> ---
>
> *Right:* A portrait of Nampeyo, holding one of her traditional pots.

POSITIVE ADVICE

"Self-pity is our worst enemy and if we yield to it, we can never do anything good in the world."

Helen Keller, deaf and blind campaigner for many progressive causes

Left: Helen Keller (left), age thirteen, with her teacher and companion, Anne Sullivan. Sullivan began working with Helen when she was just seven years old, and Keller eventually became one of the world's best-educated women.

with all these problems, some Hispanic women campaigned for better conditions for their people. In 1911, Jovita Idar and Soledad Peña organized La Liga Femenil Mexicanista (League of Mexican Feminists) in Laredo, Texas. Their aims were to protest racist lynchings, campaign for equal education for women, and help organize schools for Mexican-American children.

A CAMPAIGNER FOR THE DISABLED

In the early 20th century, one remarkable woman made an enormous difference in public attitudes toward disability. Helen Keller became deaf and blind following an illness when she was a baby. As a young girl, she was taught to use sign language by a very talented teacher named Anne Sullivan, who later became her companion. After earning a degree at Radcliffe College, Keller became a world-famous speaker and author, traveling to thirty-nine countries.

Keller campaigned for people with disabilities and supported numerous progressive causes, including women's suffrage, workers' rights, radical socialism, pacifism, and birth control. She was an inspiration to others, proving that it was possible to overcome disabilities and live a full and productive life.

CHAPTER 8

THE PERIOD IN BRIEF

I N 1920, MOST YOUNG AMERICAN WOMEN ENJOYED much more freedom than their mothers had known. They were generally better educated than the previous generation and had a far wider range of job opportunities. They wore more comfortable clothes and spent more time outside the home. Even young women from very poor backgrounds tended to have better lives than their mothers, thanks to the reforms of the Progressive Era.

Right: During World War I, it became more common for black and white women to work together. This photograph, taken in 1919, shows female workers in a navy shipyard on Washington's Puget Sound.

TURNING POINT

COSMETICS FOR WOMEN

In 1912, Elizabeth Arden (originally named Florence Nightingale Graham) returned to the United States after visiting the beauty salons of Paris. In her New York salon, she introduced her clients to a collection of rouges and tinted powders. At a time when only entertainers wore makeup, she sold lipstick, rouge, and eye makeup for ordinary women. Many older women were horrified at the thought of wearing makeup, but young women soon started to use cosmetics.

WOMEN'S WORK

Young white women living in cities could choose from a range of jobs. While some took on traditional female roles as teachers or domestic servants, others became shop assistants, clerks, or telephone operators. Middle-class girls with a college education could become doctors or lawyers, while poorer women often worked in factories. By 1920, some women had taken on traditionally male jobs as police officers, streetcar conductors, and even railroad workers.

SPORTS AND LEISURE

By the second decade of the 20th century, there were female hockey and baseball teams and women were competing in tennis and golf. Female entertainers performed as singers, dancers, and comedians. After a hard

week's work, many young women enjoyed a night out going to a local dance hall or theater or the movies.

BETTER LIVES

The reforms of the early 20th century made a difference in the lives of the poor. By 1920, most American states had laws prohibiting child labor and restricting the number of hours a woman could work. Women could find medical support when they were sick and protection from violent husbands. They even had ways to control the number of children they gave birth to.

ROOM FOR IMPROVEMENT

Despite the reforms of the Progressive Era, some women still had to cope with enormous difficulties. Many African Americans suffered from discrimination at work and hostility in their daily lives. Nevertheless, a few remarkable African-American women achieved great success, especially in the fields of business, entertainment, and sports.

By 1920, women in America had made great progress in gaining rights and respect, but they still had a long way to go. Most of the freedoms enjoyed by young women disappeared after they were married. A married middle-class woman was expected to give up her career and devote herself entirely to her husband and children. It would be at least another 50 years before women were accepted as more equal members of society.

> ### BREAKTHROUGH BIOGRAPHY
>
> **MAUD NELSON (1881–1944)**
>
> Maud Nelson started playing professional baseball at age sixteen, when she was selected as a pitcher for the Boston Bloomer Girls. She went on to play for several professional teams, including the American Athletic Girls. In 1911, Nelson became owner-manager of the Western Bloomer Girls along with her husband. In the same year, she also became a baseball scout, recruiting male and female players for professional teams. After her husband died in 1917, Nelson (who was then thirty-six years old) played again for Boston and managed a women's team for the Chicago Athletic Club. In 1923, she started the All Star Ranger Girls team with her second husband.

Timeline

1900	The International Ladies' Garment Workers' Union (ILGWU) is formed to improve conditions for textile workers. The Olympic Games include women athletes for the first time.
1901	Theodore Roosevelt becomes president of the United States. The Army Nurse Corps is formed.
1902	Helen Keller writes *The Story of My Life*, describing her experiences as a deaf and blind woman.
1903	Orville and Wilbur Wright make their first powered flight in the Wright Flyer. Jane Addams and other reformers found the Women's Trade Union League of New York. This group later combines with the ILGWU. Mother Jones leads "the children's crusade"—a strike of child workers.
1905	The Industrial Workers of the World (IWW) organization is founded in Chicago. It includes women and aims to organize all workers into "One Big Union." Edith Wharton's first novel, *The House of Mirth*, is published. Madam C. J. Walker begins selling hair-care and beauty products for African-American women.
1907	Harriot Stanton Blatch founds the Equality League of Self-Supporting Women, later called the Women's Political Union (WPU).
1908	Henry Ford launches the Model T Ford—the first car that ordinary American families can afford. The Navy Nurse Corps is formed. The first completely electric washing machine is sold. In the legal case *Muller v. Oregon*, the U.S. Supreme Court upholds Oregon's ten-hour working day for women. International Women's Day is celebrated for the first time.
1909	William Howard Taft becomes president of the United States. A group of black and white activists establishes the National Association for the Advancement of Colored People (NAACP). Women workers hold the thirteen-week "Uprising of the 20,000" in New York City.
1910	The WPU organizes its first suffrage parade in New York City.
1911	Fire breaks out at the Triangle Shirtwaist Company in New York City, and 146 workers die. Following the tragedy, 100,000 mourners march down Fifth Avenue.
1912	Elizabeth Gurley Flynn of the IWW organizes a mill workers' strike in Lawrence, Massachusetts. Amy Lowell publishes her first volume of poetry, *A Dome of Many-Colored Glass*. Juliette Low founds the American Girl Scouts movement. The Children's Bureau is formed. It conducts research into infant

mortality, child labor, childhood diseases, and sanitation.

| 1913 | Woodrow Wilson becomes president of the United States. |

Henry Ford installs a moving assembly line in his automobile factory, marking the start of a new type of factory work.

Mary Phelps Jacob invents the brassiere.

Ida Wells-Barnett founds the Alpha Suffrage Club for black American women.

Alice Paul creates the Congressional Union for Woman Suffrage (CUWS). It is reorganized as the National Woman's Party in 1916.

| 1914 | World War I begins in Europe. |

Margaret Sanger publishes *Family Limitation*, a pamphlet on birth control.

| 1915 | The Woman's Peace Party (WPP) is formed in Washington, D.C., in response to the outbreak of World War I. |

40,000 people march in a New York City suffrage parade.

Mary Ware Dennett forms the National Birth Control League (renamed the Voluntary Parenthood League in 1919).

| 1916 | Jeannette Rankin becomes the first woman to serve in Congress. |

Margaret Sanger establishes the first U.S. birth-control clinic in Brooklyn, New York. It is shut down within ten days and Sanger is imprisoned for thirty days.

| 1917 | The Russian Revolution begins. |

April: The United States enters World War I. In the following two years, nearly 13,000 women join the U.S. Navy, Marine Corps, and Coast Guard, mostly doing clerical jobs.

Alice Paul and other members of the National Woman's Party hold silent sentinel protests outside the White House. Some of them are arrested and stage hunger strikes in prison.

| 1918 | October: The annual suffrage parade in New York City is joined by women in uniform, including members of the Red Cross. |

November: World War I ends. By the end of the war, over 1,550 American nurses have served in naval hospitals and other medical facilities at home and abroad.

| 1919 | Lena Madesin Phillips founds the National Federation of Business and Professional Women's Clubs (BPW) to represent the interests of white-collar women workers. |

| 1920 | January: The 18th Amendment to the U.S. Constitution becomes law, prohibiting the sale of alcohol nationwide. |

August: The 19th Amendment to the U.S. Constitution becomes law, granting women the right to vote.

Carrie Chapman Catt founds the League of Women Voters to educate women about political issues.

Mamie Smith records *Crazy Blues*. It sells almost a million copies.

The Women's Bureau is formed to collect information about women in the workforce and to safeguard good working conditions.

GLOSSARY AND FURTHER INFORMATION

abortion An operation to end a pregnancy.

anarchist Someone who wants to change society by abolishing government and the rule of law.

astronomy The study of objects outside the earth's atmosphere, such as stars and other planets.

bail A sum of money paid as a guarantee that a person will appear in a law court on an agreed-to date.

blacklisted Banned from being a member of an organization.

blues A type of folk music developed by African Americans at the start of the 20th century.

Bolshevik A type of communist who followed the teachings of Vladimir Lenin in the early 1900s.

chromosomes The parts of human cells that control inherited features, such as eye color.

communism A way of organizing a country so that all the land and industry belong to the state and all the profits are shared among the people.

contraception The prevention of pregnancy.

diaphragm A device used by women to prevent pregnancy.

federal A system of government in which a country is divided into states, which form a union but which have independent control of their own internal affairs.

gelatin A jelly-like substance made from boiling animal bones. Gelatin is used in cooking to make jellies and mousses.

genetics The study of how individual characteristics are passed on from one generation to another through genes.

hatchet A type of small ax.

militant Aggressive and determined.

motorcade A procession of cars.

pacifism The belief that war is wrong and that arguments should be solved by peaceful methods.

pacifist Someone who campaigns to put an end to war and who aims to find peaceful methods to solve arguments.

patriotism The love of one's own country.

physiology The study of living creatures and the way they function.

picketer A person who joins a group standing outside a workplace trying to persuade other people not to enter during a strike.

Quaker A Christian group whose members reject formal services and hold meetings in which anyone may speak. Quakers often campaign for peace and social reform.

radical Thorough or extreme.

ragtime A style of jazz piano music.

reconstruction The rebuilding of a society after a disaster.

reservation An area of land that has been put aside as a place where Native Americans can live together.

rouge Pink or red makeup that some women use on their cheeks.

socialism A way of organizing a country in which the government owns the country's main industries so that, in theory, everyone may benefit from the money earned by the industries.

socialist Someone who believes that everyone in a country should benefit from the money earned by the country's industries.

suffrage The right to vote in public elections, especially elections for local and national leaders.

suffragist Someone who campaigns for the right to vote in elections.

trade union A group of workers who have organized to gain fair working conditions or pay.

unionist Someone who supports the trade unions.

urbanization The growth of towns and cities, which results in the shrinking of the countryside and the decline in country ways of life.

vaudeville A form of entertainment consisting of short acts, such as songs, dances, and comedy routines.

venereal disease The name for a range of diseases that are passed on through sexual intercourse.

workhouse A form of prison that used to exist for offenders serving short sentences. During their time in the workhouse, prisoners had to perform hard manual labor.

BOOKS

Banner, Lois W. *Women in Modern America: A Brief History*. Florence, Kentucky: Wadsworth, 2004.

Hemming, Heidi, and Julie Savage. *Women Making America*. Silver Spring, Maryland: Clotho Press, 2009.

May, Martha. *Women's Roles in Twentieth-Century America*. Westport, Connecticut: Greenwood, 2009.

DVDS

Iron Jawed Angels (HBO, 2004). Tells the story of the American women's suffrage movement, starring Hilary Swank as Alice Paul, Frances O'Connor as Lucy Burns, and Anjelica Houston as Carrie Chapman Catt.

WEB SITES

http://www.history.com/topics/the-fight-for-womens-suffrage

http://www.msu.edu/~timmnico/1910.htm

http://www.spartacus.schoolnet.co.uk/USAwomen.htm

PLACES TO VISIT

Jane Addams Hull-House Museum, Chicago, Illinois

The museum was the original "settlement house," founded in a poor neighborhood of Chicago by social reformer Jane Addams.

National World War I Museum, Liberty Memorial, Kansas City, Missouri

The museum presents the history of World War I and shows its impact on the people of the United States.

Sewall-Belmont House and Museum, Capitol Hill, Washington, D.C.

The museum is the headquarters of the National Woman's Party (NWP) and was the Washington home of the NWP's founder, Alice Paul. Its exhibits tell the story of women's campaign for the right to vote and their pursuit of equality.

INDEX

Numbers in **bold** refer to illustrations.